UNDERCOVER STORY

THE HIDDEN STORY OF

FAMILY BREAK-UPS

Sarah Levete

raintree

a Capstone company — publishers for children

Raintree is an imprint of Capstone Global Library Limited, a company incorporated in England and Wales having its registered office at 264 Banbury Road, Oxford OX2 7DY – Registered company number: 6695582

www.raintree.co.uk
myorders@raintree.co.uk

Produced for Raintree by Calcium
Edited by Sarah Eason and Jen Sanderson
Designed by Keith Williams
Picture research by Sarah Eason
Production by Victoria Fitzgerald
Originated by Capstone Global Library Ltd © 2016
Printed and bound in China

ISBN 978 1 4747 1637 6
19 18 17 16 15
10 9 8 7 6 5 4 3 2 1

British Library Cataloguing in Publication Data
A full catalogue record for this book is available from the British Library.

Acknowledgements
We would like to thank the following for permission to reproduce photographs: Dreamstime: Goldenkb 44, Kurniawan1972 43; Shutterstock: 11, 1000 Words 28, Aaron Amat 26, Orhan Cam 31, Creatista 5, 40, DFree 16, Juergen Faelchle 14, Blaj Gabriel 12, Warren Goldswain 15, Hartphotography 10, Bradley Hebdon 34, Kolessl 18, Christine Langer-Pueschel 33, Lisa S. 36, MJTH 41, Monkey Business Images 38, Yoann Morin 27, James Peragine 22, Andrey Popov 6, Pressmaster 1, 4, 42, Sergey Ryzhov 8, Tinseltown 29, Worldswildlifewonders 20, Jess Yu 24, Zimmytws 9.

Cover photographs reproduced with permission of: Shutterstock: Francis Wong Chee Yen.

Every effort has been made to contact copyright holders of material reproduced in this book. Any omissions will be rectified in subsequent printings if notice is given to the publisher.

Some words are shown in bold, **like this**. You can find out what they mean by looking in the glossary.

CONTENTS

THE TRUTH ABOUT FAMILY BREAK-UP

Single parent, lone parent, broken, **blended** – these are just some of the terms used today to describe families that result from family break-up. It is easy to label families, but it is often harder to understand the magnitude of feelings and issues that young people experience when they find themselves caught up in family break-up.

The decision to separate is never taken lightly or easily by parents because it can have such a huge impact on everyone involved, especially children. This book looks at the issues and feelings triggered by family break-up, when one parent or carer leaves his or her partner and children. It explores the often complicated and bewildering emotions that sometimes follow a break-up.

Each family member will face his or her own difficulties in adjusting to a family break-up.

BREAKING NEWS

>> According to the Office for National Statistics, the number of **divorces** in England and Wales in 2012 was 118,140, an increase of 0.5 per cent since 2011, when there were 117,558 divorces.

The book also examines the wide range of causes and effects of a break-up and possible ways to deal with this difficult situation.

GETTING THROUGH IT

There is no single or simple way to understand and manage a family break-up, or one way to cope with it. Everyone will have different experiences and different reactions.

Many people go through the storm and upset of a family break-up, but throughout the difficulties, they emerge with strong family bonds and relationships.

UNDERCOVER STORY

NO BREAK-UP

Some children live with only one parent or with relatives for reasons unrelated to the breakdown of their parents' relationship. There can be many reasons why families change, such as the death of a parent. In these situations, some of the feelings surrounding family break-up may be relevant, but there may also be different issues for those family members to come to terms with.

CHAPTER ONE

FAMILY MATTERS

Families come in all shapes and sizes. Millie lives with her mother and father. She has a younger brother. Beth lives with her stepfather, her mother, and her stepsister and brother. She stays with her father every weekend and for some holidays. Dan is 13 and lives with his mother and her new partner, who is also a woman. Farhad is 11. He lives with his aunt and uncle and their two children.

Family break-up is not easy to deal with, whatever the age of the children who are affected.

BREAKING NEWS

>> According to the Office for National Statistics, just 8 per cent of single parents in Britain are fathers living with their children.

DIFFERENT FAMILIES

Millie, Beth, Dan and Farhad all have loving families, but the families are all very different. Whatever the makeup of the family, a family should be a place of security, love and safety.

Brothers and sisters may fight, parents and children may argue, a mother or father may say embarrassing things in front of their children's friends – families have lots of ups and downs and can be very annoying at times. Despite these irritations, families are the backbone of a child's life, providing security, love, safety and a place to be oneself. That is why family break-up can be painful and traumatic, whether or not the adults involved are the birth parents, adoptive parents, stepparents or long-term partners.

UNDERCOVER STORY

CHILDREN'S RIGHTS

The international organization United Nations Children's Fund (UNICEF) recognizes the importance of family and the rights of a child to have contact with an absent parent when the parents are not living together. UNICEF states, "Children have the right to live with their parent(s), unless it is bad for them. Children whose parents do not live together have the right to stay in contact with both parents, unless this might hurt the child."

There is no right or easy way for a family to break up. It depends on each individual situation, and breaking up a family is never simple or easy. Some adult relationships end suddenly and the **couple** split up immediately. Sometimes, the couple may decide to split up and then take time setting up any practical arrangements. It can be a long time before parents make the decision to stop living together and separate. This period can be very distressing for children because they may be aware of arguments and tension, shouting or prolonged silences. They may worry about their parents' relationship.

LEGAL IMPLICATIONS

Marriage is a legally binding relationship. When a married couple separate, they can separate without going through a legal process but to end their marriage legally, they must be divorced in a **court** of law. **Cohabiting** couples can separate without finalizing the end of their relationship in law.

No two people start a relationship expecting it to end, especially when they have children.

UNDERCOVER STORY

STAY OR GO?

There is much debate in media and society about the harmful effects of family break-up. Some people believe that parents should stay together "for the sake of the children", even if the couple are very unhappy. They believe it is better for children to have two parents, whatever the situation. Others argue that it is more damaging for children to live with adults who have a very argumentative and troubled relationship. They believe that parents deserve happy, loving relationships and that it is better for children to know and experience these types of relationship than to witness an unhealthy one.

Whether or not a relationship is ended legally, any family break-up is a sad experience for all those involved.

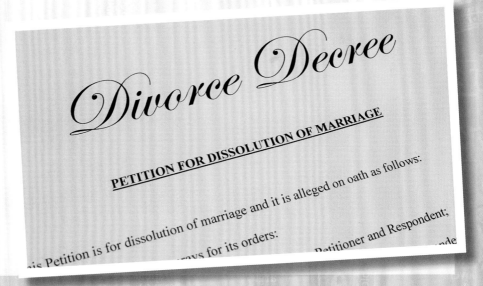

Divorce Decree

PETITION FOR DISSOLUTION OF MARRIAGE

...is Petition is for dissolution of marriage and it is alleged on oath as follows:

...ays for its orders:

Petitioner and Respondent;

CHAPTER TWO

BREAKING DOWN

Emilie and Elliot were childhood sweethearts. They had known each other for a long time. Their first child was born when they were still teenagers. Emilie left university to care for their baby. The couple worked hard to pay their bills and put down a deposit on a small house. After their second child was born, Emilie decided to go back to university to get her degree. She began to mix with a new group of people and found that she and Elliot had less and less in common. Emilie's interests changed and she wanted different things from life. Emilie and Elliot started to argue a lot and after a while, they decided it was better to live apart. Their children stayed with Emilie but continued to see their father.

Couples who marry under the age of 25 are more likely to divorce than couples who marry when they are older.

BREAKING NEWS

>> In England and Wales in 2012, the number of divorces was highest among men and women aged 40 to 44.

REASONS FOR BREAK-UPS

There are countless reasons why a relationship breaks down and parents decide to part. Problems in a relationship may develop over a long period of time and finally cause a split. Sometimes, the problem is unexpected and the break-up is sudden.

Children often want to know the exact reason why parents separate, sometimes hoping that if there is a specific problem then it can be fixed and the break-up averted. However, in many cases, there may not be one specific cause. Instead, there may be many problems that build up over time and cannot be resolved. Sometimes, there is no obvious explanation for a break-up and this can be very difficult for children to come to terms with.

Each family deals with difficulties in its own way. What leads to a break-up for one family may not cause a break-up in another – it all depends on individuals, circumstances and each unique situation.

A relationship can break down whatever the age of the partners.

All couples argue from time to time and every partnership has its ups and downs. Parents are usually able to resolve these problems. However, in some instances, the arguments only seem to get worse and the parents grow angrier and more distant from each other. Sadly, this can lead to a break-up.

People fall in love and sometimes they fall out of love, for no particular reason. One parent may meet someone else and, over time, decide to live with him or her. However, it is important to remember that when a parent stops loving his or her partner, it does not mean he or she no longer loves their child or children.

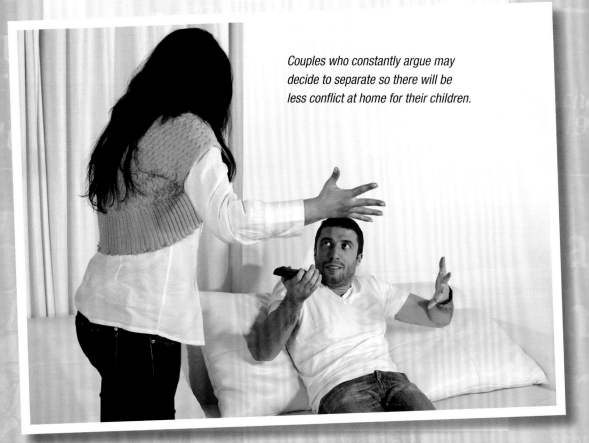

Couples who constantly argue may decide to separate so there will be less conflict at home for their children.

BREAKING NEWS

>> In the United Kingdom in 2012, one in seven marriages ended as a result of adultery.

UNDERCOVER STORY

DIPS AND DIVORCE

Money worries can put a strain on relationships. However, reports show that the divorce rate falls when a country's economy dips, and rises when its economy improves. Could this be because of the financial consequences of running two households in the event of a divorce and the cost of hiring solicitors to legally end a marriage?

UNDER PRESSURE

Stress and worry can make a person moody and difficult to live with. He or she may become withdrawn or lack interest in others. A person who suffers from **depression** or another mental health issue often finds it difficult to be involved and engaged with family activity. This behaviour can put a huge strain on the other parent, who takes on the responsibility of dealing with the family alone. One parent may find a partner's drug or alcohol **abuse** too harmful and difficult to cope with and reluctantly decides to separate.

Many parents argue about money – what should be spent on what or whom and how much! They may have different views about which expenditures should be given priority. These disagreements can expose even deeper cracks in the relationship, cracks that the parents may feel unable to repair.

The terrible truth is that some adults are **abusive** towards their partner or child. This abuse can take many forms. It may be physical violence, sexual abuse or psychological bullying. None of these forms of abuse is acceptable. In cases of abuse, a child should try to find a trusted adult with whom he or she feels safe.

The child can then be given the support and attention he or she needs to be safe from harm.

FEARING A BREAK-UP

Children may worry that telling someone about abuse will lead to the break-up of their family. However, it is much more important for children to find the support and safety they need and deserve than to risk their physical or emotional well-being in an attempt to hold their family together. Children who are exposed to family violence may well suffer from depression and then later become victims or abusers in their adult relationships. Of course, many children are able to recover and are not affected in this way at all.

It is frightening and upsetting for children to be aware of or witness, violence or abuse towards one of their parents.

Children often feel intense anxiety and fear when one dearly loved parent is being abused. They may feel guilty for not interfering and trying to stop the abuse, or they may feel guilty for still loving the violent partner. No child should have to experience that kind of dilemma.

It is important for children to be able to talk to a trusted adult about any abuse they see at home.

UNDERCOVER STORY
HARD TO LEAVE

People sometimes wonder why an abused parent does not simply leave a violent household. In reality, it is often very hard for the victim to leave. She (and less often, he) may fear that her safety and that of her children will be threatened even more if she leaves. The abusive partner may control the household's finances, leaving the abused partner with no money or shelter if she attempts to leave. Thankfully, there are now organizations that work to protect the well-being of people fleeing **domestic abuse**.

CHAPTER THREE

WHAT HAPPENS DURING BREAK-UPS?

Lila was five and George was 12 when their parents decided to live apart. For a few months before his parents announced their **separation**, George had retreated to his room most evenings to avoid being caught up in another fight. He loved both parents, but he hated the way they treated each other. George became sullen and quiet. He felt that his parents were not explaining their relationship issues to him and were treating him like a small child, even though he knew there was a serious problem.

Many people manage to separate and still maintain a friendship. Gwyneth Paltrow and Chris Martin have "consciously uncoupled" but remain friends and committed to joint parenting.

When George's parents told him and his sister they were going to live apart, he felt overwhelmed. Thousands of questions flooded his mind: where would he live and, more importantly – who would he live with? What if he had to live with one parent and Lila with the other? What about his birthday, which was only a few weeks away – who would give him his present? And what about school – would he and Lila have to move to another school?

DIFFICULT TIME

Family break-up is part of a long and difficult process and there are many complex issues to consider. For young people this process can feel overwhelming, especially if the parents are preoccupied, unhappy and do not seem to be dealing with any of the practical problems their children are rightly concerned about. There are so many questions young people want to ask, and need answers to, during a family break-up, but frustratingly the answers are not always clear-cut.

HITTING THE HEADLINES

ARRANGEMENTS AFTER BREAK-UPS

According to some reports, actress Katie Holmes took Tom Cruise completely by surprise when she left him, taking their daughter with her. However, despite the difficulties, the celebrity couple managed to separate and divorce within 11 days. They came to an **amicable** agreement about the **custody** of their daughter, access rights and how their considerable fortune was to be split. This speedy settlement was arranged with the services of hugely expensive solicitors. Most divorces take much longer to arrange.

One of the first things young people often wonder when their parents are separating is "Who will live with whom?" Parents often make the decision about living arrangements and children may feel this resolution is very unfair. Should a child be given the right to decide with whom he or she lives? This is a difficult question and one for which there is no easy answer. Ideally, parents will take a child's views into account, but it may not always be possible or in the best interests of the child to act on those views. Each situation is different and parents will try to come to the best arrangement for their children.

It is not always easy, but it is important that both parents try to keep up strong relationships with their children.

BREAKING NEWS

>> The Office for National Statistics says that one in three children live without their father.

USUAL OUTCOMES

Children are more likely to stay with their mother, although many children do live with their fathers. Sometimes, parents agree on joint parenting. In this case, the children live with one parent and regularly stay with the other. This arrangement is called **shared parenting**. It means children spend time with both parents. Shared parenting is not always the easiest option – it means two bedrooms, two toothbrushes and often two sets of rules as children split their time between two homes.

Sometimes, custody is awarded to one parent alone, with the other parent having little or no access to the child or children. In these instances, the parent may not be in a position to care for his or her children. This inability to care for the children can be for a variety of reasons. For example, the parent may have an alcohol or drug problem that needs to be dealt with before he or she can safely care for a child once more.

UNDERCOVER STORY

THE FATHER'S ROLE

Some **campaign** groups, such as Fathers4Justice, protest against judgements by family courts. The fathers in the campaign groups believe that too many decisions are made in favour of mothers and that the fathers' importance in their children's lives is not sufficiently recognized. Sometimes, these campaign groups use stunts such as dressing up in superhero outfits and hanging from cranes to raise awareness of their cause.

Divorcing or separating parents can usually come to an agreement about the care of their children, who are, after all, the most precious part of their family. However, in some instances, this resolution is not possible. At these times, parents may go to the courts to ask for help in making decisions about child custody arrangements or access to their children. In these cases, the needs of the child should be at the forefront of any decisions about contact with parents. In some cases, a court will grant a parent only limited contact with his or her child. This decision may be related to safety issues or other concerns. It is not always easy for family members to accept such decisions.

The case of Halle Berry and her partner Gabriel Aubry highlight the difficulty of agreeing on custody arrangements when one parent wants to move abroad.

CAUGHT IN THE MIDDLE

Mediation can often be used to help people to avoid the trauma and cost of going to court. In these cases, a professional acts as a "middle person" between the parents and tries to help them put aside arguments and anger. Instead of shouting, the parents are encouraged to come to an agreement that is in the best interests of their children.

When parents argue over access or custody, children often feel torn between the two people whom they love the most. Parents may say unkind things about each other to their children or try to influence their views. This behaviour is unfair – the relationship breakdown is between the adults, not the children. Children should be able to love both parents without fear of upsetting one or the other.

HITTING THE HEADLINES

MOVING FAR AWAY

In one high-profile case in 2012, actress Halle Berry wanted to move to France with her young daughter and French partner, to whom she is now married. The daughter's father, Canadian Gabriel Aubry, opposed the move because it would prevent him from maintaining a face-to-face relationship with his child. After a custody discussion, a judge decided that Berry could not move to France. Resolving custody and access arrangements becomes very complex when the parents live in different countries.

Change seems to affect everything when a family breaks up. There can be emotional upheaval and confusion, but there are also a lot of practical changes to make and adjust to. It often seems to young people that the changes affect them the most, without them even wanting the changes or being given any choice about what happens to them.

In time, both parents may need to leave the family home and live in new places. This relocation may mean moving away from an area. If a parent moves a considerable distance, then young people may have to change schools. This relocation can be a hard blow, forcing young people to leave their friends when they most need them. However, relocating can be a good opportunity to make new friends and people can keep in touch with old ones, too.

It is important to keep up everyday activities, even when everything else is changing.

SIBLINGS

Every child in the family will feel differently about their parents' separation. One child may feel angry if a brother or sister seems to be siding with one parent. It is natural to have conflicting reactions, but it is important to respect each other's viewpoint and to show each other understanding and support.

IMPACT ON PARENTS

The impact of separation and divorce is hard on parents, too. What was once a shared daily responsibility between two parents becomes the responsibility of just one parent. This can be very difficult and the parent left with the daily care of a child or children may not always get it right. This change can be particularly challenging when there are very young children to care for.

UNDERCOVER STORY

SOME THINGS DON'T CHANGE!

When family break-up takes place, it is important to remember that it is the situation that changes, not the people. Friends, family and brothers and sisters remain the same. Physical distance does not break friendships or relationships. It does require flexibility, however, and it means finding new ways to keep in touch. Thankfully, today's technology means it is easier than ever to maintain regular contact with friends who can offer the support young people need at this challenging time.

CHAPTER FOUR

FAMILY BREAK-UP HURTS

Joe felt as if his world had collapsed. His mother was leaving. Both parents were unhappy, angry and distracted. Joe could not take in what was happening. He was worried about his exams – they were taking place really soon – but no one else seemed to have even thought about that. Joe felt angry, but he also thought he was being selfish and did not want to upset his parents any more. He was sick of his younger brother asking him questions about what was happening – Joe did not have the answers to those questions! For a while, Joe felt as if his head would explode with the confusing rush of feelings he was experiencing.

At first, it can feel overwhelmingly hard to deal with parents' splitting up but it does get easier with time.

HITTING THE HEADLINES

GIRL POWER!

Multi-award-winning singer, Adele, was born in Tottenham, London. Her father left the family home when she was just three years old. Adele says that she was encouraged to sing by her mother, Penny. The singer has a close relationship with her mother – about her she said, "My mum's quite arty – she'd get all these lamps and shine them up to make one big spotlight." When Adele won six Grammy awards, the first person she thanked was her mother, saying, "Mum, your girl did good! I love you."

Joe kept out of the house as much as he could, staying instead with friends. With chaos at home, Joe felt that normal rules no longer counted. His schoolwork no longer seemed so important, either. He started spending time with a new crowd and smoking cannabis.

OVERWHELMING FEELINGS

Young people like Joe often feel overwhelmed when parents split up. Adults are making the decisions about their relationships with one another, but it is the children who have to come to terms with the separation of those they love the most.

Young people may think they are being selfish if they wonder and worry about which parent is going to come to parent-teacher meetings at school or with whom they will spend Christmas. This is quite natural and it is okay to ask parents these questions.

Parents going through a separation or divorce are often sad and distracted, at the very time when children most need love and support. Understandably, the children may feel that they no longer matter, but this is not the case. For a while, children may feel very lonely and find it hard to continue with everyday activities. However, talking to others can help to put upsetting feelings **into perspective**. The good news is that the difficult feelings, no matter how painful they are, do pass in time.

CONFUSING FEELINGS

Children often feel let down and betrayed by the very people who are meant to provide them with security and love. As a result, it is natural to feel anger, hurt and sometimes even hatred. It helps to remember that parents never make the decision to part lightly – they have often taken a long time to come to their decision, and have realized that they will be better parents if they are happier apart from each other.

Young people sometimes feel guilty because they may think that their behaviour led to their parents' break-up. It is important to remember that the child is not responsible for the relationship breakdown and adults have reasons for separating that have nothing to do with the children.

It is common for young people to feel angry with their parents and the world around them.

HITTING THE HEADLINES

STAYING STRONG

Bradley Wiggins is one of the greatest ever cyclists. While racing in the 2012 Tour de France, Wiggins tried to think of things to make him cycle harder to win. He said, "I was just thinking back to my childhood, my father leaving us when I was a kid, growing up with my mum and then my grandfather brought me up, he was my father, my role model. He died when I was on the Tour two years ago."

Bradley Wiggins, here in the yellow jersey, was raised by his mother after she left his abusive father, who was an alcoholic.

Life as a teenager is about growing up, becoming more independent and discovering your identity as a young adult. It is an exciting time, but not always an easy one, because it may be packed with emotional and physical turmoil. An adolescent likes his or her home to be a place of stability and security. When a parent leaves, a teenager becomes very upset.

REACTING TO THE HURT

A teenager can feel abandoned and rejected when a parent leaves. Feeling confused and unhappy, the teenager may try to ignore these emotions and "switch off". He or she may become withdrawn or try to separate from the upset by using drugs or alcohol. Reliance on such substances may help a person forget his or her troubles in the short term, but it inevitably leads to worse and more damaging problems. A young person may feel angry and begin to behave badly. Without the support of two parents, he or she may start to act in a more aggressive or **rebellious** way.

When a parent leaves, a child can feel rejected. This feeling of abandonment can lead to angry and rebellious behaviour.

BREAKING NEWS

>> Almost half (48 per cent) of couples in the United Kingdom divorcing in 2012 had at least one child aged under 16 living in the family.

Some teenagers will blame themselves for their parents' problems and direct their anger towards themselves.

From anger and hatred to sadness and despair, the feelings surrounding family break-up are very painful but also very natural. They will pass in time, but talking about them can also help to prevent these feelings from leading to harmful behaviour and other problems.

Many people, like Harry Styles, come to terms with the hurt of parents breaking up.

HITTING THE HEADLINES
FEELING HURT

Harry Styles of the boyband One Direction has spoken about his parents' divorce, "When I was seven, my mum and dad divorced and that was quite a weird time. I remember crying about it. I didn't really get what was going on properly. I was just sad that my parents wouldn't be together any more."

Keeping in touch with both parents is important for children, but sometimes it may not be easy or even possible. If one parent moves away, it may be difficult for him or her to maintain contact with children. However, after a separation or divorce, it is often possible for children to keep in touch with the absent parent – even if the adults are not currently speaking to one another.

CONTACT AND CHALLENGES

Sometimes, a young person may choose not to keep in touch with a parent, perhaps because he or she feels too angry and hurt about the break-up. Even if a child feels this way, he or she may still have strong, loving feelings towards the absent parent and may miss him or her. This confusion of feelings can be difficult to understand. In time, the young person may decide to renew communication and the parent and child may develop a strong and loving relationship once more.

UNDERCOVER STORY

GRANDPARENTS' LOVE

Grandparents do not stop being grandparents just because their son's or daughter's relationship breaks down. They continue to love their grandchildren and want contact with them. However, it may not be easy for them to see their grandchildren regularly, particularly if their son or daughter does not have **joint custody**. If parents stop grandparents from seeing their grandchild, the grandparents may be left with no choice but to seek a court order to allow visits.

It is not just the relationship with the absent parent that presents challenges. The parent with whom children live most of the time is usually responsible for the most difficult aspects of parenting, such as telling children to tidy up rooms, do homework and stick to rules. It is easy to feel frustrated and angry with this parent because they present children with irritating rules and often daily friction.

Young people sometimes swing back and forth between feelings of love, sorrow, anger and hatred for each parent. This perplexing mix of feelings does become less raw and acute as time moves on, and children can gradually find new ways of communicating with and loving both parents.

Grandparents and other relatives can continue to be a great source of support for children.

CHAPTER FIVE

MOVING ON

Trudie was living with her father and his new partner, who were expecting a baby. Fourteen-year-old Trudie was trying to come to terms with the whirlwind of changes that had affected her – her mother had left home to live with a new partner, then her father had quickly dated and found a new partner. Nothing seemed the same to Trudie.

Even her relationship with her beloved father was different. They now argued about who should do the household chores – and Trudie had never done household chores when her mother lived at home. She and her father even argued about room changes to make space for the new baby. Trudie's friends were a huge support to her because they behaved

UNDERCOVER STORY

MOVING FORWARD

Coming to terms with family break-up means moving on. This moving forwards does not mean forgetting the absent parent or loving him or her any less. It just means going on with one's life. Sometimes, a young person may even feel relieved that his or her parents have separated or may feel indifferent to the change in the family. It is understandable to feel this way and it does not mean a child does not love or care for his or her parents.

BREAKING NEWS

>> In 2012, according to the Office for National Statistics, 19 per cent of men and women divorcing had their previous marriage end in divorce.

normally and treated her in the same way they had before her parents separated. At first, Trudie gave her stepmother a hard time, challenging her every decision. Trudie's stepmother also found it really hard to know what to do – she did not want to replace Trudie's mother, but she also felt that she needed to build a healthy and loving relationship with her stepdaughter.

It is not easy to get used to new family setups.

LEARNING TO ACCEPT CHANGE

Change can be hard. Unwanted change is particularly hard to deal with. The process of adapting to new situations takes time and people will inevitably experience confusing and conflicting feelings along the way.

The change in one family is often the beginning of another, new family. This may be exciting, but it can also be daunting for everyone involved and new families present particular challenges for children.

It is not easy to accept a mother or father meeting and dating a new partner. Children often feel strongly that their parent should stay single – they may hope for their parents' reconciliation and a new partner puts an end to that hope.

When two families come together, there are a lot of new adjustments for everyone to make. Developing strong family relationships takes effort and time.

BREAKING NEWS

>> According to reports, nearly one-third of families in the United Kingdom include a stepchild from a previous relationship.

HITTING THE HEADLINES

STEP STEREOTYPES

Stepfamilies have received particularly bad press in literature. Just think of Cinderella's cruel stepmother and taunting stepsisters or Snow White's jealous stepmother. It is not easy for any woman or man to take on the role of stepparent. He or she may not have had experience with children and may be very worried about forming relationships with the children of a new partner. Accepting a stepparent does not mean a child is being disloyal to the natural parent – it just means they are learning to manage new relationships.

Things can be complicated if a new partner was the cause of the parents' separation. The children might feel very hostile and resentful towards the new adult in their lives.

NEW RELATIONSHIPS

When a new partner comes onto the scene, it is easy for a child to compare him or her to the absent parent – often unfavourably! However, these feelings can usually be overcome if the new partner tries to build his or her own relationship with any children, rather than try to replace a much-loved parent.

Blended or stepfamilies often come with stepbrothers or stepsisters, which means getting along with yet more people. Children may find themselves sharing their home and parent with other children whom they hardly know. Such relationships take time to adjust to. Talking calmly and honestly about feelings can help to prevent a buildup of bad feelings.

Almost 2 million children live in a family where one parent is not their own.

Running a household on just one income is much harder than it is when two adults are contributing to the budget. There is often less money to live on and the family may need to move somewhere where living costs are cheaper.

Parents who split up often continue to argue about money and how much money each parent should put towards the costs of raising children and running a home. One or both parents may be in new relationships with their own stepchildren and money may be tight.

Some parents take on more work to pay the bills.

BREAKING NEWS

>> According to the UK charity, Gingerbread, paid work is not a guaranteed route out of poverty for single parent families.

TOUGH TIMES

Single parents often have to work long hours to earn enough money to pay a mortgage or the rent, to pay bills and buy food and clothing for their children. This work schedule often means they have less time to spend with their children. This lack of time can be extremely difficult for the parent, who misses his or her children and may feel guilty that he or she is not spending more time with them. It is also difficult for the children, who need attention and love from their parent. The children may also feel unhappy because things seem to be getting harder rather than easier now that their parents have separated. Talking to parents can help to make everyone aware of the challenges that individuals face – and help everyone to see things from a different point of view.

UNDERCOVER STORY

GIFTS FOR LOVE

Parents who do not live with their children for the majority of the time may try to make up for the lost time by giving their children a lot of gifts. This can cause resentment with the other parent. It does not improve the lives of the children, either. Although children love gifts, they usually prefer to have quality time with their parent, spending time together and talking.

The poverty rate for children in single parent families where the parent works part-time is 30 per cent. It is 22 per cent where the parent works full-time.

Young people cannot fix their parents' relationship, but they can help to take control of the way they handle a family break-up and look after themselves. Focussing on positive activities, such as meeting friends or playing sports, can help them to forget about their problems for a while.

It is important to be open and honest about feelings. However, it is understandable if young people do not want to talk to their parents. They may feel that talking to one parent would be disloyal to the other. They may feel guilty about resenting their parents. They may also feel just too angry to talk to them. Talking to friends or trusted adults can help to bring a sense of perspective to an upsetting situation. There are often school counsellors who can offer support and advice, too.

It is good to forget about family problems and have fun with friends.

FAMILY SUPPORT

Aunts, uncles, other relatives, and family friends often want to help and offer support to children going through family break-ups. However, it is not helpful if they say unkind and hurtful things about one of the parents involved! It is perfectly fine for children to ask them not to criticize the parent.

Some young people might feel jealous of friends whose parents are still together. They may feel angry that their parents are not able to get along as well as other people's parents who have separated. Every family is different and comparing them will not help to establish new and lasting relationships in the changed family.

UNDERCOVER STORY
CHANGING RELATIONSHIPS

People do not forget or "get over" it when parents separate, but they can come to terms with the break-up and find ways to establish positive, new family relationships. Relationships change all the time. A family break-up forces people to establish different kinds of relationships with parents and it can be an opportunity to make stronger, better relationships. Adjusting to change is not easy and it takes time. In some break-up cases, young people find that their parents are much happier apart and this optimism makes everyone's relationships easier and more positive in the long term.

CHAPTER SIX

ATTITUDES TO FAMILY BREAK-UP

After the social revolution of the 1960s, some couples began to live together without marrying. However, up until the mid-1990s, it was still unusual for a couple to live together unless they were married and it was very unusual for a child's parents to be unmarried.

Today, families may have one parent, stepparents, two mothers, two fathers ... The family setup is much more flexible, but no less important. It is essential that people show respect and consideration for each type of family.

In the past, some people faced hostility if they did not conform to traditional family stereotypes.

Today, there is much more acceptance of different family setups than there used to be. What is important is that family members show each other kindness and support, and children, whatever the family's structure, feel secure, safe and loved.

BREAKING NEWS

>> In 2012, there were 5.9 million people cohabiting in the United Kingdom – this is double the 1996 figure.

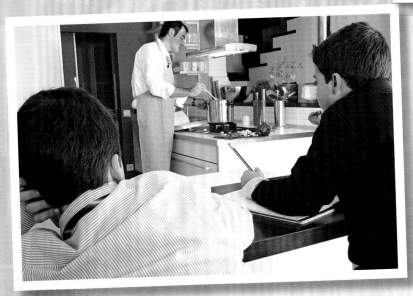

*The changing face of families means challenging traditional **stereotypes.***

UNDERCOVER STORY

UP AND DOWN

In the 1970s, in many countries there was a rise in the number of divorces. There were several possible reasons for this rise. Changes in the law made it easier to get a divorce. Women began to earn more money, so with more financial independence they could realistically consider supporting their family alone. While the rate of divorce in some countries, such as the United Kingdom, has risen, in other countries, including the United States, the divorce rate is falling. This drop could be because fewer people are marrying and many cohabit instead. It could be because many couples decide to settle down together when they are older and these relationships tend to last longer. There are many ways to interpret the figures on family break-up, but what matters most is that in each family, children are loved, cared for and safe.

Newspaper headlines sometimes scream that single parent families are responsible for many social problems, from social unrest to low achievement in school. There is often a lot of negative press around "broken" homes, which are regularly blamed for the behaviour of unruly children. These negative stereotypes are not helpful.

BRINGING UP A FAMILY

Bringing up children is hard, but it is even harder when there is only one parent to support and care for the children. It is also extremely difficult to bring up children in a family in which both parents live together, but constantly fight and argue.

Just because a child has experienced family break-up, it does not automatically mean that he or she will suffer at school or later in life. Nor does it mean that the child will turn to drugs or alcohol. Any of these things can happen to anyone, regardless of his or her family setup.

Children from any and all types of families can achieve success and happiness.

More important than any family arrangement is the love and support a child receives from his or her home and from the parent or parents with whom he or she has contact.

President of the United States, Barack Obama, is proof that a broken home is no barrier to achievement and happiness in any walk of life.

HITTING THE HEADLINES

MAKING IT

Barack Obama's parents separated when he was two years old. At the age of 10, he went to live with his grandmother, who then brought him up. Obama went on to twice become president of the United States. His example proves that a child who has experienced family break-up will not necessarily turn out to be troubled.

FAMILY BREAK-UPS – THE WHOLE STORY

Nothing can take away the upset and hurt caused by shattered families. However, there are ways to rebuild and re-form families and develop even stronger, more positive relationships.

There is undeniably a lot of heartache and distress for young people when their parents split up, but this suffering does pass and those involved do recover.

Family break-up can be an incredibly painful process, but it is important that children and young people realize that it can lead to strong, positive and loving relationships within new family setups.

POSITIVE STEPS

No one would wish the upset and hurt of a family break-up on anyone, but the new family structure can support secure and caring relationships and positive things do emerge. Children and young people learn to manage changing situations and this knowledge can make them mindful and sensitive individuals.

It is important for children to talk about how they feel to trusted adults and friends. Talking about feelings can help to make things clearer and it aids children in feeling less confused and lonely.

Finding ways to cope with and adjust to family break-up does not happen overnight – it is all part of a gradual journey. There will be many opportunities to repair and build relationships with both parents and new family members.

UNDERCOVER STORY

NO GOOD TIME

There is no right or wrong time for parents to part. Young children may be less aware of what is happening when their parents split up, but when they are older it can take some time to come to terms with their experience. Some children may have spent most of their time with only one parent before a break-up, so they do not experience the direct sense of loss that many children feel when one parent leaves. However, they may still need to deal with their feelings about why their parent was not involved in their lives before the break-up and since. The effect on adult children can be difficult, too, even though they live away from their parents and possibly have their own children. Family matters at every age. When the family changes, it causes ripples and waves that can make a difficult ride.

GLOSSARY

abuse physical or emotional harm

abusive causing physical or emotional harm

amicable friendly

blended mixed together. When one family joins with another, the combined, new family is often described as "blended".

campaign fighting for rights

cohabiting living together without being married

couple two people in a relationship

court place where a judge makes legal decisions about issues and conflicts

custody responsibility for looking after a child

depression mental illness where the person feels persistently sad for weeks or months

divorce legal ending of a marriage

domestic abuse physical or emotional harm by one person in a marriage or cohabitation

into perspective comparing a situation to give a clearer, more accurate point of view

joint custody situation in which both parents are given custody of a child

mediation professional support for couples who are splitting up to help them do so with as little conflict as possible

rebellious resisting authority and rules

separation when a couple splits up

shared parenting situation in which a child splits his or her time between both parents

stereotype fixed way of thinking about a person

FIND OUT MORE

BOOKS

Family Break-Ups (Talk About),
Sarah Levete (Wayland, 2009)

Family Crisis (Emotional Health
Issues), Jillian Powell (Wayland, 2013)

It's Not the End of the World,
Judy Blume (Atheneum Books
for Young Readers, 2014)

ORGANIZATIONS

Family Lives
Helpline: 0808 800 2222
Website: **www.familylives.org.uk**
Family Lives is a charity that helps
parents to deal with the changes that
are a constant part of family life.

Relate
Helpline: 0300 100 1234
Website: **www.relate.org.uk**
Relate is the United Kingdom's largest
provider of relationship support.
Each year, the charity helps more than
1 million people who are struggling
with relationship problems.

Fathers4Justice
Fathers4Justice is a campaign
organization that aims to highlight
the "injustice" often experienced by
fathers during divorce proceedings:
www.fathers-4-justice.org

Gingerbread
Gingerbread offers single parents and
their children support:
www.gingerbread.org.uk

INDEX